LEADERNETICS
IMAGES AND INSIGHTS FOR
CULTURE-SHAPING YOUNG LEADERS

STUDENT EDITION

JEFF GALLEY & STEPHEN BLANDINO

ABOUT THE AUTHORS

Jeff Galley is the president of Nexlead, an organization dedicated to enabling young leaders to change the future of society. He has fifteen years experience in developing young leaders through coaching, training, and travel expeditions. Jeff lives in Texas with his wife Christy and their three children.

Stephen Blandino is the associate pastor at Christ Church in Fort Worth, Texas, where he provides oversight to small groups, adult discipleship, and leadership development. In addition, he equips leaders through training events, coaching and consulting, and the development of leadership resources. Stephen lives in Texas with his wife Karen and their daughter Ashley.

Scripture taken from THE MESSAGE. Copyright ©1993, 1994, 1995, 1996, 2000, 2001, 2002. Used by permission of NavPress Publishing Group.

Scripture taken from the HOLY BIBLE, NEW INTERNATIONAL VERSION. Copyright ©1973, 1978, 1984 International Bible Society.

Used by permission of Zondervan Bible Publishers.

ISBN: 0-9711942-6-2
Library of Congress Control Number: 2006920428

TABLE OF CONTENTS

Foreword / 5
What Is a Leadernetic? / 7

UNIT ONE: BEGINNING THE LEADERSHIP JOURNEY
Chapter 1: Finding Your Place of Leadership / 11
Chapter 2: Thinking Like a Leader / 17

UNIT TWO: ESTABLISHING THE CREDIBILITY TO LEAD
Chapter 3: Being a Leader of Character / 25
Chapter 4: Being a Great Listener / 29
Chapter 5: Building Trust With Others / 33

UNIT THREE: LEADING YOURSELF (BEFORE YOU LEAD OTHERS)
Chapter 6: Developing Self-Discipline / 39
Chapter 7: Learning to Set Goals / 45
Chapter 8: Managing Your Time / 51

UNIT FOUR: BECOMING A LEADER IN STEP WITH GOD
Chapter 9: Building Your Life and Leadership on the Bible / 59
Chapter 10: Being a Leader In Step With God / 65

UNIT FIVE: EMBRACING THE INGREDIENTS TO LEADERSHIP GROWTH
Chapter 11: Identifying Your Leadership Strengths / 73
Chapter 12: Developing a Personal Growth Plan / 79
Chapter 13: Finding a Leadership Coach / 85

UNIT SIX: USING YOUR LEADERSHIP TO MAKE A DIFFERENCE

Chapter 14: Being a Culture-Shaping Leader / 93
Chapter 15: Making Courageous Leadership Decisions / 99
Chapter 16: Sharing Christ With Others / 103

Notes / 107

FOREWORD

As a student leader, I have always noticed that we young leaders want to improve the quality of our leadership ability and also have fun in the process. What if I told you that you could accomplish all of this with Leadernetics? As mind-boggling as it may seem, Leadernetics has done that for me.

In today's fast-paced society, we are constantly bombarded with tons of images—quick commercial bites, flashing internet images, and the constant motion of video games. Leadernetics applies that visual approach to learning leadership by using hand-drawn images to represent leadership principles. Each image, easy to draw and understand, will help you learn important leadership principles in a way that really works.

I was first introduced to Leadernetics on a travel expedition with Nexlead. Ever since, the images have stuck with me because they go hand in hand with real-life leadership experiences that I face every day. In fact, I couldn't tell you the number of times I've thought back to things like "The Moment of Choice" when faced with a decision, or "The Weekly Meeting With Yourself" when I need to better manage my time. These pictures will change the way you view leadership, too.

Keep this book with you in your backpack so you can make the most of *Leadernetics*:

- Use *Leadernetics* to introduce a leadership truth to a friend.
- Review the images when you have a spare minute—that way you're keeping them fresh in your mind.
- Refer back to a Leadernetic when you're going through a similar situation in real-life.

I have been learning about leadership from Nexlead for several years, and I can say Nexlead is changing the face of leadership training. So get ready for a fun and innovative journey!

—Elizabeth Hundley

WHAT'S A LEADERNETIC?

If you are like thousands of other students today, you want to use your passions to make a difference. You want to do something that changes your world, or maybe even the whole world. We have written *Leadernetics* to provide you with a path to be that kind of leader!

What is a "Leadernetic" anyway? A Leadernetic is a leadership concept presented in the form of an image that can be drawn by hand. You will read a chapter each week, then your teacher, parent, or mentor will draw the image for you to copy into your book. He or she will then teach a full lesson on how to put the leadership insight represented by the image into practice in your life.

The fact that all of these leadership principles are presented in the form of an image is important for two reasons. First, the image helps you to better understand a leadership principle. Second, the image will stick in your mind and will remind you to live out the leadership principle. Here's what a few students who live by Leadernetics have to say:

> *"Leadernetics helps me to visually experience a leadership lesson. Months later the images and insights are always still very much with me."*
> —Whitney

> *"I like Leadernetics because I can carry it around and look through the images to remember what I need to focus on."*—Dumont

> *"Leadernetics is awesome! Every day I face something that I can tie to a Leadernetic. It has helped me grow tremendously."*—Leslie

> *"Leadernetics helps me grasp relevant leadership concepts. And it is a simple tool for teaching leadership principles to others."*—Aaron

> *"Leadernetics puts leadership into visual images that are conducive to my personal growth. It helps me to strengthen my weaknesses while maintaining my strengths."*—Michelle

"Leadernetics gives me a quick leadership lesson that is easy to remember. Each one is very thought-provoking and makes it easy for me to teach what I learn to others."–Jacqui

"Leadernetics helps me to visualize the concept, which makes it easier to understand. Every leader can draw something out of each image."–Will

"I found that using Leadernetics helps me follow the leader (Jesus) and become a better leader in life situations."–Heather

The first unit of *Leadernetics* will get you started on your leadership journey. You will identify your place of leadership and learn to think and act like a leader. The second unit will help you establish the credibility to lead by being a person of character and by gaining respect and trust from others. The third unit will help you develop the ability to lead yourself by setting goals, being self-disciplined, and managing your time. The fourth unit will help you understand the importance of cultivating a healthy relationship with God by building your life and leadership on the Bible and learning to walk in step with Him. The fifth unit helps you engage in ongoing personal development by identifying your leadership strengths, developing a personal growth plan, and finding a leadership coach. And the sixth unit will empower you to influence your world by becoming a culture-shaping leader, making courageous leadership decisions, and sharing your faith in Christ.

If you work hard at learning and living these principles, you will take giant steps forward in your leadership ability. Carry the book with you, and review your Leadernetics often. Share them with others. And use them as a guide for your leadership for a long time to come!

—Jeff Galley and Stephen Blandino

UNIT ONE:
BEGINNING THE
LEADERSHIP JOURNEY

1 FINDING YOUR PLACE OF LEADERSHIP

"Passion, though a bad regulator, is a powerful spring."
—Ralph Waldo Emerson—

THE LEADERSHIP SPRINGBOARD

Notes about this Leadernetic:

_____

_____

_____

_____

_____

_____

_____

_____

_____

Do you wonder how to get started in leadership or where you should be leading? Have you ever asked, "Don't I need a position before I can begin to be a leader?" Or maybe right now you don't even care about becoming a leader!

Before we begin to answer these and other questions about getting started in leadership, read the following two leadership profiles:

LeighAnna Hutchinson had cancer when she was six years old, so she is passionate about helping other kids who have cancer. During her seventh-grade year at Seabrook Intermediate School in Seabrook, Texas, LeighAnna organized a benefit walk that raised more than $10,000 for the Candlelighters Foundation, a group that supports pediatric cancer patients and their families. LeighAnna found a place to lead based on her passion to help other kids with cancer.[1]

Nathan Sloan has a passion to help others through the use of law. "I am currently an intern at the American Center for Law and Justice, where we recently had a very important case in which I was able to conduct research that was later used by our counsel in his oral argument before the Supreme Court." Nathan will complete undergrad school in a couple of years, then plans to enroll in law school. Nathan has found a place to lead based on his passion for law and justice.

Did you notice that both LeighAnna and Nathan became leaders because they pursued something they were passionate about? That's where leadership begins.

PASSION IS THE STARTING POINT OF LEADERSHIP

You've heard from an early age that it's important to control your passions, which is very true. For example, you shouldn't just run up and kiss a guy or girl you think is attractive. And you shouldn't haul off and punch someone when they make you mad. But there is another side to passions.

Your passion will reveal where you should lead–God has given you certain interests. It's within these areas of interest, or passions, that you should be leading. These are the kind of passions you do want to act on! Don't lead in areas where you don't have an interest. Lead within your passions.

Maybe for you it's sports, or academics, or perhaps music. Or perhaps it's helping the poor, fighting AIDS, or solving another problem you see. And passions can also be tied to a career field such as business, politics, education, or many others. Your passion will reveal your unique place to be a leader—and in a very real sense it's a calling from God to be a leader in a specific area.

Your passion will keep you committed—Leadership is hard work and requires a ton of commitment. You are much more likely to remain committed to something if you feel passionate about it. Nobody has to motivate you in those areas because you are naturally passionate about them.

Your passion will help your leadership mature over time—As you grow older and gain more experiences in life, you will become passionate about different things. As your interests grow, your opportunity to be a leader will also expand. If you continue to adjust your leadership roles as your passions and interests grow in the future, you will be more likely to find long-term success because you will be in step with God as He has placed those passions within you.

HOW TO DISCOVER YOUR PASSIONS

Your passions already exist; they don't have to be created. You just have to stop and notice what they are. Consider the following pointers as you identify just what it is that "fires you up."

Notice what you are good at doing—Discovering your passions begins by realizing what you are naturally good at doing. Think about the things you do that generally go well. It's very likely that you have some natural abilities in those areas. And chances are you will feel pretty passionate about it as well.

Ask key questions that will cause you to focus in on your passions—Spend some time (either alone or with a trusted friend or mentor) considering the following questions:

- What meaningful activities do you enjoy spending time doing?

- If you had $500 to do something in your community, how would you spend it?

- What experiences (good or bad) have most shaped your life?

- What issues in the news seem to get your attention the most?

Come in contact with things that will stir your passion—You never know when a passion might be lying dormant within you. Reading books, listening to interesting people, watching the news, browsing the internet, and volunteering for new experiences may uncover something you never knew would get you fired up!

HOW TO TURN YOUR PASSIONS INTO LEADERSHIP OPPORTUNITIES

Passion doesn't do much good unless you put some action behind it, like LeighAnna and Nathan did in their areas of passion. You have to turn your passion area into an opportunity for leadership.

Get involved in your passion area—Don't try to take action in everything that interests you—that's impossible. Choose one or two areas and commit yourself to being involved in them. And be intentional about finding a place to get involved both inside and outside your church so your passion and influence can be used to make a difference in your community.

As you think about college, begin to make career choices based on what you are passionate about. In a sense, your passion for a certain career is a calling from God, and He will work through you in that career field to make a difference in society.

Begin to act like a leader in your passion area—If there is a leadership position open, apply for it. But holding a position isn't required in order to be a leader in your passion area. Just begin to "act" like a leader (the next chapter will give you some pointers on how) by putting your strengths and abilities to use and by looking for ways to serve others.

Work hard to develop your leadership skills—Excelling as a leader in your area of passion is going to require that you work diligently to develop the five basic skills of a leader. If you mix together these skills with your passions, you will begin to see your leadership expand rapidly. These skills are:

- Creatively solving problems
- Communicating with others
- Working with a team
- Planning a project
- Managing your time

Taking the time to identify ways to turn your passions and interests into leadership opportunities is your first step in becoming a leader, and ultimately in living a life that makes a difference.

You naturally excel in the areas for which you have a passion, so it's fair to assume that if you lead in your passion area you are going to be good at it. And leading in your passion area will give you a purpose because you are doing something that's important to you!

LIVE THE LEADERNETIC

1. What are the reasons that it's important to be leading in something you feel passionate about?

_____

_____

_____

2. Passions aren't created; they already exist. How does a person go about identifying his or her passions?

_____

_____

_____

3. There are five key leadership skills that a leader needs to develop in order to be an effective leader. What are they?

_____

_____

_____

2 THINKING LIKE A LEADER

> "A leader is someone who helps
> improve the lives of other people."
> —Sam Ervin—

THE LEADERSHIP LENS

Notes about this Leadernetic:

_____

_____

_____

_____

_____

_____

_____

_____

_____

As a regular citizen, Esther was chosen to become queen because of her remarkable beauty. She served for several years as the queen before her leadership, prompted by a crisis, began to kick into gear. The crisis emerged because Haman, the king's second-in-command, determined to destroy all the Jews. He manipulated the king into ordering their execution in cold blood. Esther's cousin, Mordecai, challenged Esther to look at what was happening through the "leadership lens" when he learned of the plot to kill the Jews. He said to her, "Who knows, maybe you were made queen for such a time as this?" (Esther 4:14). In other words, he was saying, "You have been put here for a reason... now go do something about it!"

Esther (who was also a Jew, although the king didn't know it) suddenly understood that it was up to her to do something. She had a purpose to fulfill—to save her people—and she decided to do something about it. She mustered up enough courage to walk in uninvited to meet with the king (which in her day could have gotten her killed) and request that he attend a dinner that she had prepared for him. The dinner gave her an opportunity to spill the beans about Haman's evil plot to destroy all of the Jews. The king reversed the decree that all of the Jews be killed, and instead had Haman killed. Esther saved her people.

 Austen Hamilton is a fifteen-year-old student who lives in Ohio. Like almost every student in the world today, Austen spends a lot of time on the internet and was faced with the overwhelming amount of obscenity and lawlessness there. Austen decided to do something about it, so he put the wheels in motion to introduce something called the Internet Bill of Rights to lawmakers in Washington. Within a few months Austen found himself challenging several hundred students to be a part of his drive at the 2004 Youth Summit in Cleveland, Ohio.

 Ella Gunderson became frustrated trying to find something fashionable—yet modest—in a world where she felt surrounded by immodest clothing for girls. So she wrote a letter and sent it to the corporate office of Nordstrom's. Here's part of what she said in her letter: "Dear Nordstrom," she wrote. "I am an eleven-year-old girl who has tried shopping at your store for clothes (in particular jeans), but all of them ride way under my hips, and the next size up is too big and falls down. I see all of these girls who walk around with pants that show their bellybutton and underwear," she continued. "Your clerks suggest that there is only one look. If that is true, then girls are supposed to walk around half-naked. I think that you should change that."[2] The company executives wrote back and said that they were already considering adding new lines of clothing that were more modest, and her letter confirmed the need for new styles. The next season new styles began to appear in their stores.

JUST WHAT IS LEADERSHIP, ANYWAY?

Leadership is using your influence to help people and change society. Esther, Austen, and Ella each give us a snapshot of leadership. They didn't hold a position or title, they simply chose to do something about what they observed.

Within your areas of passion there are things that can be done to make a difference. Many students just coast along, but leaders choose to notice and react to the world around them.

LEADERS LOOK AT THE WORLD FROM A DIFFERENT PERSPECTIVE

Leadership is who you are and what you do, not a position you hold–You don't have to gain a title to become a leader. Leadership begins within you. It's a change in perspective you decide to take on, then it's followed by doing things that a leader should do. In fact, sometimes people who hold a leadership title aren't really leaders at all, because they have not taken on the perspective of a leader.

When you begin to solve problems and help people, others will begin to see you as a leader–Before you know it, opportunities will begin to open up for you. Others will begin to follow you, and your level of responsibility will increase. Here's a point to consider: If others aren't treating you like a leader, perhaps it's because you are not acting like one.

CHANGE THE WAY YOU LOOK AT PROBLEMS

Rather than complaining about (or ignoring) problems that you notice around you, you should see them as opportunities to do what leaders do–solve problems! Taking responsibility to get things done will earn you respect from others, especially if you are willing to solve the problems that others may ignore.

Deal with problems before they become a crisis–Most problems are ignored unless they are easy to solve or if they become a crisis. One of the smartest moves you can make is to become a problem-solver. Be willing to stick your neck out on the line to make things happen.

Take initiative to do something that others may be ignoring–When you see an opportunity to do something that needs to be done, do it, even if it's not necessarily a problem. This is a perfect opportunity to be a leader. Take the initiative, while others around you might be too focused on themselves to do so.

CHANGE THE WAY YOU LOOK AT PEOPLE

If you want to be a great leader, you have to realize that leadership is not about you. It's about what you do for other people.

Make others around you the center of attention rather than yourself–Instead of asking, "What can you do for me?" you need to begin asking, "What can I do for you?" In fact, this perspective is the essence of charisma. You don't need an outgoing personality to have charisma. If you make others the center of attention they will want to be around you, which makes you a charismatic person.

Look for ways to simply make life better for others–Leaders are always finding ways to improve the quality of life for others, even if it means hard work and sacrifice. That's what Esther, Austen, and Ella did in the leadership profiles you read at the beginning of the chapter.

Respond quickly when you see others being treated unjustly–It's your job to deal with injustice. When you see others being treated wrongly in your community, on your campus, or anywhere in the world, it's your job to do something about it.

In chapter 1 you identified where you should be leading by getting a clear idea of your passions. Now you have learned how to be a leader in that area—by solving problems and helping people in your area of passion. Both of these principles work hand-in-hand. If you live them out, your ability to lead will begin to rapidly accelerate!

LIVE THE LEADERNETIC

1. What is the definition of *leadership?*

   _____
   _____
   _____

2. What two things can you begin to do that will make you a leader, even if you don't hold a position or title? Give an example of how you can do both of these within your area of passion.

   _____
   _____
   _____

UNIT TWO:
ESTABLISHING THE
CREDIBILITY TO LEAD

3 BEING A LEADER OF CHARACTER

"Character is power; it makes friends, draws patronage and support, and opens the way to wealth, honor and happiness."
—**John Howe**—

CHARACTER AND INFLUENCE

Notes about this Leadernetic:

_____

_____

_____

_____

_____

_____

_____

_____

_____

Aspire for great character! "Don't lose a minute in building on what you've been given," Peter says in 2 Peter 1:5-8. "Complementing your basic faith with good character, spiritual understanding, alert discipline, passionate patience, reverent wonder, warm friendliness, and generous love, each dimension fitting into and developing the others. With these qualities active and growing in your lives, no grass will grow under your feet, no day will pass without its reward...." Peter was clear about it—work hard to have great character.

Imagine that leadership is like a ladder. Like any ladder, this "leadership ladder" has two legs. One leg represents *competency*, which is another word for leadership skills and abilities. The other leg represents *character*, which is your moral and ethical strength. You may develop your competency to a great extent, but without the character to match it your leadership will fall—the same way a ladder with one leg can't stand up.

STRONG CHARACTER IS A LEADERSHIP ACCELERATOR

Authors James Kouses and Barry Posner have surveyed over 20,000 people on four continents to identify the top qualities that people would like to see in their leaders. Number one? Honesty. This character trait ranked higher than other characteristics such as forward-looking, inspiring, and competent![3] The truth about leadership is that others care more about how you lead than anything else—they expect you to be a leader of character.

If you have character, others will want to follow you—You might be able to force others to follow you because of your position, knowledge, or power. But if you have character, people will want to follow you, knowing you are honest, trustworthy, and will treat them with respect and honor.

If you have character, God will open opportunities because He trusts you—If your character is solid, God will open up more leadership opportunities for you because He trusts you. You may think the key to reaching leadership greatness is to achieve something worth noting. But God doesn't measure greatness based on your accomplishments. He defines it based on the depth of your character.

HOW TO WORK WITH GOD AS HE SHAPES YOUR CHARACTER

Just a few years ago, Kaliel Tuzman was quite literally on top of the world. His internet business was booming, and his personal net worth had climbed to 70 million dollars even before he reached his thirtieth birthday. But then the bottom fell out. When his company hit the wall, he not only lost all of his wealth but also landed about one million dollars in debt. Kaliel is very open about the fact that this painful crisis was his life's most poignant character-growth experience. On one hand, the pain of losing all he had accumulated was unbearable, but it was also the pain that sparked within him significant character growth. He now says that he is a better man because of the pain he had to endure. Just like Kaliel, God is working in your life to develop character.

Respond the right way to the circumstances of everyday life–Just like Kaliel Tuzman, you are going to experience many things in life that have the potential to dramatically develop your character. If you will learn to respond to the challenges of life in a positive way, your character will begin to mature.

- *Pain:* God doesn't create pain in your life, but He does use it as an opportunity to develop who you are. If you get angry and bitter when times are tough, you miss the chance to grow. On the other hand, if you trust in God and keep your attitude straight, the strength of your character will increase.

- *Tests:* God will test your obedience regularly. When you have a chance to cheat, will you do it? When you have a chance to be dishonest, will you? When you are told to do something, will you follow through? Each time you do the right thing your character grows; each time you don't, it takes a step backward.

- *People:* God uses people who sharpen your character. Are you willing to be submissive to your leaders? How do you respond to difficult people–do you treat them poorly in return? If you treat people with respect and honor when it would be easier not to, then your character takes a step forward.

If you blow it, don't despair; get ready for another chance soon–You are not always going to do the right thing when God uses His character-shaping tools in your life. Don't panic when you blow it. God's grace is very big, so He will give you another chance very soon to do the right thing. Be on the lookout for another opportunity right around the corner.

With character, your leadership will always be growing and accelerating. This is true no matter where your area of leadership might be–at home, on campus, in the community, or on the job. Commit to working

with God as He shapes your character, enabling you to be the leader that
He has called you to be!

LIVE THE LEADERNETIC

1. What is the definition of *character*? How is it different from
competency?

   _____

   _____

   _____

2. Why are others more likely to follow you if they feel that you
are a person of character?

   _____

   _____

   _____

3. What are the three "tools" that God uses to develop your
character?

   _____

   _____

   _____

4 BEING A GREAT LISTENER

"When I am getting ready to reason
with a man, I spend one-third of my
[time thinking about myself and what I]
[am going to say, and two-thirds about]
him and what he is going to say."
—**Abraham Lincoln**—

AN OPEN EAR

Notes about this Leadernetic:

_____

_____

_____

_____

_____

_____

_____

_____

_____

Stephen Covey, in his classic book, *The Seven Habits of Highly Effective People*, coined the phrase "seek first to understand, then to be understood." But the natural tendency of many young leaders is to "seek first to talk, then pretend to listen!" It's true that one of the greatest ways to influence others is through communication, but that doesn't necessarily mean talking.

According to Proverbs 18:2, what you say is not the starting point for good communication. The secret is actually found in how well you listen to and understand what others have to say. "Fools care nothing for thoughtful discourse," it says. "All they do is run off at the mouth." Then, just a few verses later, Proverbs 18:13 says, "Answering before listening is both stupid and rude."

Jason works as an advisor at a state university, and part of his job is to enroll students in classes for the semester. One student was having a bad day and took her frustration out on Jason. Although he was being verbally attacked, Jason remained friendly, kept a helpful attitude, and was willing to listen to the student's needs. This calmed the student, and Jason was able to reassure her that everything would work out. Not only did that student make it a point to be nice to Jason in the future, but Jason's supervisor noted his excellent interpersonal skills and passed on his positive impressions of Jason to others in the department.

Before others will pay attention to what you say, they have to feel confident that you have first heard and that you understand their point of view. So when it comes to communication, listening carries more weight than talking. There are few things that build credibility and respect faster than learning to be a good listener.

WHEN YOU LISTEN, OTHERS WILL RESPECT YOU

Listening gets you past the mind and into the heart—When the person speaking senses that you genuinely care about what they feel, you have won over their heart. This allows you to connect with them on a much deeper level than just words and intellectual exchange.

Listening ensures that others will take to heart what you say—When others know you care about what they feel, they will return the favor and care about what you have to say. Your words will mean much more to them. So the key to getting others to hear what you have to say is to first want to hear what they have to say!

HOW TO BE A BETTER LISTENER

Most people listen only with the intent to reply to what the other person is saying. But great communicators take time to not only hear, but truly understand what the other person is saying, and it enables them to communicate much more effectively. The following pointers will help you become a better listener.

Ask good questions–Learn to ask questions when you are initiating any kind of conversation. Doing so will get the other person talking right away, and it will communicate that you care first about what they think and feel. Be sure your questions are open-ended and cannot be answered with a short response.

Closed question: Did you have a good day?

Open question: What was the best thing about your day today?

Closed question: Do you think this is a good idea?

Open question: What are your thoughts about this idea?

Repeat back the essence of what you hear–As you are listening to someone speak, take time to pause and reflect back to them the essence of what they are saying to you. This enables the person speaking to understand that you are truly listening to what they have to say.

> *Example:* If a friend is telling you about a problem they are having with a project at school, you might say, "So, your biggest headache right now is this project at school, right?"

Listen for the "message behind the message"–Great listeners are not just hearing the words someone is saying. They are trying to understand the feelings behind those words. If you can recognize the way someone feels, that will give you access to their heart. Words come from the head, feelings come from the heart.

> *Example:* The person in the last example who is having trouble with a project at school is probably feeling stressed or frustrated. If you acknowledge that feeling, they will realize that you care about them.

Leaders who listen to others are the most respected and most effective. In fact, the first step in servant leadership is listening–hearing and perceiving what another person needs, and then doing something about it.

LIVE THE LEADERNETIC

1. What are the two reasons that listening is such a powerful communication skill?

_____

_____

_____

2. What are the three things that you can do to improve your listening skills? Give an example of each.

_____

_____

_____

_____

5 BUILDING TRUST WITH OTHERS

"Trust men and they will trust you; treat them greatly and they will show themselves great."
—Ralph Waldo Emerson—

RELATIONSHIP SUPERGLUE

Notes about this Leadernetic:

_____

_____

_____

_____

_____

_____

_____

_____

_____

_____

Leadership isn't something you do on your own. Leading means that you lead, serve, and work alongside others. "It's better to have a partner than go it alone," Solomon says in Ecclesiastes. "Share the work, share the wealth. And if one falls down, the other helps, but if there's no one to help, tough! By yourself you're unprotected. With a friend you can face the worst. Can you round up a third? A three-stranded rope isn't easily snapped" (Ecclesiastes 4:9, 10, 12).

If you can't lead on your own, that means you have to have relationships with others—and those relationships have to be strong. Trust is the most important ingredient to strong and lasting relationships. It's like Superglue—it creates a powerful bond between you and others that will last, remaining strong through anything that your relationship might face.

LEADERSHIP, RELATIONSHIPS, AND TRUST ALL GO TOGETHER

You can't lead without relationships—Did you know that 85 percent of the reason that people get a job, keep that job, and become successful in that job has to do with how well they can work with others? Your ability to foster meaningful relationships and work as a part of a team also affects your leadership ability far more than technical skills, intellectual ability, or knowledge.[4] Your ability to work with and lead others is largely dependent on how well you can build relationships.

You can't have relationships without trust—What is the key to being a winner at relationships? Lou Holtz, former head football coach at the University of Notre Dame, nailed the answer when he said, "When someone meets you, that person first wants to know one thing: Can I trust you?" Trust is an incredibly powerful tool. If you let your guard down and trust others, then they do the same, the bond between you grows to be very powerful. Trust is like Superglue to relationships.

HOW TO BUILD TRUST WITH OTHERS

There is a story told by author Tim Hansel about himself and his son, Zac. They were out in the country, climbing around in some cliffs. Tim heard his son's voice from above yell, "Hey Dad! Catch me!" He turned around to see Zac jumping off a rock straight at him. Zac had jumped first and *then* yelled. Tim caught his son, then both of them fell to the ground, stunned. Tim explained, "When I found my voice again I gasped in exasperation: 'Zac! Can you give me one good reason why you did that?' He responded with remarkable calmness: 'Sure... because you're my dad.'" Zac jumped into his dad's arms, almost without warning, because he trusted him.

When others trust you, they'll be willing to follow you where you want them to go because they know that you're looking out for their best interests. The following suggestions will give you some practical ways that you can build that kind of trust with others.

- Be comfortable with yourself and don't try to impress others.

- Listen to the ideas and opinions that other people have.

- Let people get to know the "real" you, and share your honest opinions.

- Give others the benefit of the doubt without jumping to conclusions.

- Admit it when you make a mistake, and accept apologies from others.

- Don't try to control everything; let others make decisions.

- Ask for help when you need it.

- Look forward to spending time with people.

WHAT TO DO WHEN TRUST GOES WRONG

Superglue is powerful, but it can also be dangerous. Like the girl who glued her lips together, thinking a small bottle of Superglue was actually lip balm, or the woman who used Superglue to apply false eyelashes (she probably didn't score high on the genius scale). Then there are the poor guys at a British McDonald's who got stuck to a toilet seat that someone had poured Superglue all over. It took five hours to get him free.

Trust is much the same. It's a powerful tool, but it can also be dangerous if someone uses it in an incorrect manner. There will be times when others take the trust you build and turn it against you. When this happens, don't just throw the relationship out the door. Take the initiative to deal with the conflict and restore the relationship.

Don't react in an emotional way—Stay calm and get the facts. Don't freak out. Tell the other person how you feel without getting angry or emotionally out of control. If you react the right way from the beginning, it's likely that you'll be able to repair the damage to your trust and move on.

Be willing to forgive, yet insist on dealing with the issue–Don't be hesitant to hold the other person accountable for what they have done to you. Just do it with respect and treat them with dignity, even if they have not done so with you. If the other person isn't willing to make things right, then there is nothing you can do. But if they are willing to apologize, be willing to forgive them and move forward.

Take time to slowly rebuild trust–Trust is like water in a cup. When someone pours some of it out, it has to be replaced before the trust is regained. This doesn't happen overnight so be patient, and be willing to work at it over time.

Trust (both trusting others, and being a trustworthy person) must be a part of your journey of leadership. Without it, you will not be able to gain followers. With it, others will want to go where you are going.

LIVE THE LEADERNETIC

1. How are leadership, relationships, and trust related to each other?

   _____
   _____
   _____

2. List the eight ways that a leader can build trust with others.

   _____
   _____
   _____
   _____

3. If a breakdown in relationships and trust occurs, how should you respond?

   _____
   _____
   _____
   _____

UNIT THREE:
LEADING YOURSELF
(BEFORE YOU LEAD OTHERS)

6 DEVELOPING SELF-DISCIPLINE

> "He who reigns within himself and rules passions, desires, and fears is more than a king."
> —John Milton—

THE MOMENT OF CHOICE

Notes about this Leadernetic:

_____

_____

_____

_____

_____

_____

_____

_____

_____

Self-discipline is the ability to lead yourself. Before you can lead others, you have to learn to lead yourself; in other words, you must have self-discipline. When you are in control of your time, passions, health, and commitments you will find that leading others will follow more naturally. Why? Because you, yourself, are the hardest person to lead! So seek first to win the "self-leadership" challenge.

One way to quickly lose respect from others is to not exercise self-discipline. According to Proverbs 25:28, "A person without self-control is like a house with its doors and windows knocked out." Not many people want to buy a house that is in obvious disrepair. A homebuyer will pass right over a house that has not been cared for and will choose to buy a house that has been properly maintained. Likewise, if you don't have self-discipline, you will be passed by when it comes to leadership opportunities.

 Ignatius Loyola (1491–1556) is one of history's most remarkable leaders. In his younger years he was quite a rabble-rouser and troublemaker. Then at the age of thirty he found himself fighting in the Spanish army against the French. During the battle he was hit with a cannonball, badly injuring both of his legs. The French army captured him, but because they were so impressed with his courage during the battle they took him back to France to recuperate instead of throwing him into prison. During his time of recovery, he was given a book to read about the life of Christ. He was so moved by the book that he immediately converted to Christianity, and over time his passions for romance and conquest were forged into an iron-willed, loving, and God-honoring leader. Loyola founded the Jesuits, who for nearly 500 years have not only been meeting the practical needs of literally millions around the world, but have also educated some of the world's greatest leaders in the church, government, sciences, and other fields. His positive impact on the world is undisputed. Loyola held a very unique approach to leadership. He believed that the hardest person to lead was himself. Loyola believed that if he could master the challenge of self-leadership (otherwise known as self-discipline) then God would be free to work through his life in boundless ways. Loyola was absolutely right on target! If you can learn to tell yourself what to do, then you will gain the momentum you need to not only move forward in life, but also to lead with strength and purpose. Self-discipline is a critical aspect of leadership.

The apostle Paul, like Loyola, also learned the importance of self-discipline. "I don't know about you," he says in 1 Corinthians 9:26–27, "but I'm running hard for the finish line. I'm giving it everything I've got. No sloppy living for me! I'm staying alert and in top condition. I'm not going to get caught napping, telling everyone else all about it and then missing out on it myself."

LEADERSHIP REQUIRES THAT YOU TAKE INITIATIVE

No one is going to force you to do the important things of "self-leadership." You have to take the initiative.

You have to follow through on your goals–No one else is going to force you to follow through on the goals that you set, yet your leadership effectiveness depends on it. If you want to be a leader who makes a difference, you have to learn to follow through.

You have to do the right thing when put to the test–When life puts you to the test, when you have a chance to choose right or wrong, what will you do? No one is going to be twisting your arm, and God won't force you to stand up for truth and be courageous. It's your choice.

You have to be known as trustworthy and reliable–You cannot build a reputation of trust based on the reputation of another person. You have to demonstrate to others that you are one who can be trusted. Being viewed by others as a person who is trustworthy is certainly going to require self-discipline.

HOW TO DEVELOP SELF-DISCIPLINE THROUGH THE MOMENT OF CHOICE

Self-discipline is all about making decisions. The key to developing more self-discipline is to learn to make good decisions at the moment it counts the most. The following three practical steps will help you expand your self-discipline.

Clarify the area in which you tend to be undisciplined–When you are lacking in self-discipline, you have to be clear on where your self-discipline is lacking before you can correct it. Identify the area where things are going wrong, and determine that you are going to work on it.

For example, if you have trouble getting homework in on time, it may be that you are spending too much time sending IMs or watching TV, so you don't have time for homework. The real issue isn't that you don't do your homework, it's that you spend too much time on other things.

As you evaluate your level of self-discipline, consider the following areas where it is particularly important for you to exercise self-discipline as a young leader:

- Health and fitness

- TV and the internet

- Getting out of bed on time

- Setting aside time with God and for Bible study

- Properly following through on commitments and assignments

Identify the precise point where things usually go wrong–Once you have determined where you need to develop more self-discipline, your next step is to identify the exact point where things go wrong when your self-discipline fails. Getting yourself to think differently requires that you know where things are going wrong. Essentially, you want to "track back" to find the point where you are making a decision that gets you off track.

For example, if you set your alarm but don't get out of bed when it goes off in the morning, there are several possible places that could be the moment of choice. It may be that your problem is that you stay up too late at night and don't get enough rest. Then when the alarm goes off the next morning your body screams, "I need more sleep!" so you don't get out of bed. No matter how hard you try, you will have trouble getting out of bed unless you go to bed on time. So your moment of choice is not at the point when the alarm goes off, it's when you decide to stay up too late the night before.

Then again, it may be that you are going to bed on time but you just love to sleep. So your moment of choice is when the alarm clock goes off. That is the moment to choose whether you want to lead yourself or not.

Decide ahead of time what you will do when you hit that point again–Now that you know the decision point, focus your energy on that specific moment. Rehearse in your mind before that moment arrives what you will do. Ask God to help you find the inner strength to do the right thing.

When you get one small win, it will build your confidence and inner strength. Focus on winning once, then again, and before you know it you will have conquered your problem area. Then you can apply that same muscle to developing self-discipline in another area of your life.

MORE HINTS ON HOW TO IMPROVE YOUR SELF-DISCIPLINE

In addition to finding your "moment of choice" these four ideas will help you improve your overall level of self-discipline:

Practice doing small things that you are reluctant to do–Every day, find something you don't like to do and force yourself to do it. In our culture, we are told all of the time that you don't have to do what you don't want to do. Reverse that thinking by training yourself to do what you are reluctant to do. It will build your self-discipline "muscles."

Get the hard things out of the way first–If you have a list of things to do, do the tough things first. It will feel good to get them done, then you can look forward to things that are easier. If you save the hardest thing to do for last, you will be more likely to procrastinate.

Resist the idea that you have to be constantly entertained–Set aside times when you teach yourself to not be entertained. Set aside a few hours each week when you don't use your computer, don't watch TV, don't talk on the phone, and don't read. Use that time to creatively use your mind. This will teach you to increase your ability to think and act on your own.

Finish one thing before you move on to another–Having too many things going on will make you feel frustrated, and it will make your mind feel scattered, which will increase the chances that you will drop the ball on something. Finish one project or assignment before you start another.

Putting effort into developing your self-discipline will really pay off! Proverbs 16:32 says that "moderation is better than muscle, self-control better than political power." Now that's a bold statement!

LIVE THE LEADERNETIC

1. What is *self-discipline*?

_____

_____

_____

2. In what areas should you take initiative on your own as a leader?

_____

_____

_____

_____

3. What are the three steps to developing more self-discipline in your life?

_____

_____

_____

_____

7 LEARNING TO SET GOALS

"People with goals succeed because they know where they're going."
—Earl Nightengale—

FUTURE TENSE

Notes about this Leadernetic:

_____

_____

_____

_____

_____

_____

_____

_____

When it comes to planning ahead, every personality is different. Some people naturally love to "shoot from the hip" and just let things turn out any which way. Then others are all about planning—they love lists, goals, and always know exactly where they are headed.

Regardless of the kind of personality you have, the old saying is true: "If you fail to plan, you are planning to fail." And your credibility will grow faster if you follow through on your commitments and fulfill your promises. So no matter what kind of personality you have, it's important to learn to look ahead and set goals.

Harvard University conducted a ten-year study that monitored graduates of an MBA program from 1979 to 1989. The study found that ten years after graduation only 3 percent of the students were consistent goal-setters. But that 3 percent who were setting goals were making ten times as much money as the other 97 percent combined.

LEADER PROFILE Afton Grossardt, 17, of Wrangell, Alaska, a senior at Wrangell High School, played a key role in founding and developing the Wrangell Youth Court, a judicial system run entirely by young people that tries and sentences juveniles accused of first-time offenses. Since the program began, juvenile crime has declined 25 percent in Wrangell! Afton began working on the project three years ago, seeing it as a way to "help middle- and high-school students learn from their bad choices, and spur them to become better people." It took about two years for Afton and other interested students to draft a course curriculum, write bylaws, apply for grants, hire a coordinator, train new members, and recruit adult volunteers from the community. Afton was one of the first to pass the Wrangell Youth Court bar exam and now serves as both a judge and an attorney on cases. Afton's dream and commitment required that he set and follow through on goals. Without goal-setting he would have never launched Youth Court, and the crime rate would have never dropped 25 percent.

God is in favor of thinking ahead. He wants to be in charge of your work, but He also assumes that you will use wisdom and diligence by making solid plans. Check out what He has to say in Proverbs regarding making plans:

- "Put God in charge of your work, then what you've planned will take place."–*Proverbs 16:3*

- "Refuse good advice and watch your plans fail; take good counsel and watch them succeed."–*Proverbs 15:22*

- "Form your plans by seeking counsel, then carry it out using all the help you can get."–*Proverbs 20:18*

EMBRACE A FORWARD-THINKING MINDSET

Before you can be an effective goal-setter, you should begin by simply developing the habit of thinking ahead. The best way to think ahead is to often ask the following two questions:

What do I need to get done this [month, semester, year, etc.]?–If you don't think ahead about assignments and responsibilities, they will catch you off guard, and you will be late or won't do a good job getting them done. Great leadership demands that you think ahead about what needs to be done.

What kind of person and leader do I want to be?–Remember that, although God has placed within you the potential for leadership, you have to take the responsibility to develop that potential to its highest level. Developing your leadership skills doesn't happen by accident, it happens because you first identify exactly how you want to grow as a leader.

SET GOALS THAT WILL TAKE YOU TO A DESTINATION

But just asking "future tense" questions isn't enough. Based on where you want to be and what you need to accomplish, write down your goals. A well-written goal matches the five following characteristics (these make the acronym SMART).

Goals should be:

Specific–Don't be vague about setting your goals. Write them out in detail. Be precise. It will help keep you focused and clear on exactly what needs to be done.

Measurable–Be sure that you make your goal measurable so that you can keep track of your progress and evaluate whether or not it was accomplished.

Achievable–Don't try to take on too much, yet make your goals big enough to make you work hard at achieving them. You want to find a balance between the two.

Relevant–Be sure that your goals will actually lead toward your future aspirations. There's nothing more frustrating than to achieve a goal, only to discover that it was leading you in the wrong direction.

Time-bound–Set a deadline to accomplish your goal. If you don't, it's possible to procrastinate until the goal never gets accomplished.

- Examples:

    Poorly-written goal: I want to be a better leader.

    Well-written goal: My goal is to be more confident in the way I interact and converse with others by this time next year.

    Poorly-written goal: I am going to apply for a grant.

    Well-written goal: My goal is to obtain a grant for my new community program by June of next year.

FOLLOW THROUGH ON YOUR GOALS

The goals you set are worthless if they are not acted upon. These suggestions will help you follow through on your goals:

Make a list of action steps needed to reach your goal, beginning with the end and working backward–Smart planning always begins with the end in mind, so work your way backward. List all of the major things that must be done in order to reach your goal. It's possible that one goal may have several action steps.

Assign a due date to each action step–Decide when each of your action steps must to be completed. Write the due date next to each action step so you will know when it needs to be done.

Write all your action steps down on a to-do list that you will refer to each week–You have taken a goal, broken it down into smaller steps with deadlines, and now you have a "to-do" list. In the next chapter you will learn how to look at your to-do list each week and decide what needs to be done.

Thinking ahead and setting goals should be a simple habit. Don't overcomplicate it, yet be consistent. Setting goals will help you reach your dreams this year and over your lifetime.

LIVE THE LEADERNETIC

1. What two questions will give you a forward-thinking mindset?

   _____

   _____

   _____

2. What are the characteristics of a well-written goal?

   _____

   _____

   _____

   _____

3. What can you do to ensure that you follow through on your goals?

   _____

   _____

   _____

   _____

8 MANAGING YOUR TIME

"Don't start your week until you've
finished it on paper first."
—**Jim Rohn**—

THE WEEKLY MEETING

Notes about this Leadernetic:

_____

_____

_____

_____

_____

_____

_____

_____

_____

I magine that you receive a letter in the mail today from the lawyer of a distant relative who has died and left you a large amount of money—$525,600 to be exact. The letter says that you will get your money one day at a time over the next year. Every day exactly $1,440 will be deposited into your bank account for a total of $525,600. Just imagine what you could do with more than a half a million dollars! But, there's a catch. (You knew it was too good to be true, didn't you?) At the end of the day, whatever you don't spend is removed from your bank account, and the next day you would begin with a fresh $1,440. Getting all of the money will mean that you have to choose every day how to use it. You would surely find some very creative things to do with all of that money to be sure that none of it went to waste.

Now, come back to real life. Every day you are given 1,440 minutes to use however you choose. Like the money from your relative, at the end of the day the minutes are gone and can never be regained again. If you don't choose to spend your time wisely, your life will be rushed, others won't be able to count on you, and you will fall short in accomplishing your own personal goals and dreams.

Even Jesus had to choose how to use His time. He told his disciples in John 7:6, "'The right time for me has not yet come; for you any time is right'" (NIV). Like Jesus, if you will develop the habit of choosing how to spend your time you will be dependable, trustworthy, and will live a life that makes a difference. And you will have plenty of time left over to include the fun things in life—like hanging out with friends, watching movies, and PlayStation 2.

 Elyse Moni is very busy. She is into sports and theater, but perhaps her biggest time commitment these days is helping other teenagers, like herself, who live and struggle with obsessive-compulsive disorder (OCD). She was diagnosed with OCD when she was eight years old, and as a teenager she began to notice when other teens were struggling with the same problems. So Elyse started a webzine and a support group for OCD teens. She manages a newsletter with constant deadlines and schedules the support group meetings on a regular basis. For Elyse, time management is key to keeping things moving in the right direction.[5]

CONTROL YOUR TIME IN SEGMENTS OF ONE WEEK

If you don't deliberately choose to control your time, it will control you. The best way to control your time is in segments of one week.

Thinking a week at a time breaks your life into manageable segments–Sometimes the idea of managing your time wisely can be very daunting. Don't try to become an expert at time management–just begin to think one week at a time, and you will be surprised at how well things go.

Thinking a week at a time gives you flexibility with your schedule–Thinking in segments of one week allows you to be flexible. And if you have a week or two where you are disorganized and lazy, you always know you can start fresh the next week.

GATHER THE TOOLS FOR TIME MANAGEMENT

Before you can begin to manage your time each week, you have to get the basic tools of time management in place. Many people over-complicate time management. But all you really need to get started are the following three things:

An *organized room*–If all your school and work information is cluttered, your mind will also be cluttered. Putting the following three things in place will help you get and stay organized:

- *Start an inbox:* Your inbox is a place to put papers, school work, pictures, mail, or anything else you want to keep. Instead of letting these things pile up and scatter, keep them in one place.

- *Set up some files:* Get a filing drawer or use a box to hold your files. Label a set of manila folders by alphabet, and put them into the files. This will give you a place to store things you need to use at a later date without having to create piles of stuff in your room.

- *Set up email files:* Instead of keeping all of your emails in your "inbox," set up several other file folders in your email system to keep emails that you don't want to delete.

A *master "to-do" list*–You need a way to keep track of your various things to do. Those small, yellow sticky notes will get lost, and your mind can only remember a certain number of things to do before you forget. Three ideas you might consider as you plan to keep track of things to do are:

- A PDA (such as a Palm Pilot)
- Computer software (such as Outlook or Word)
- A notebook (good ol' fashioned paper!)

Any time you are assigned something to do (at school, work, or home) always record it on your master to-do list, along with the date it is due.

Don't forget to include the action steps that you created when setting goals (in chapter 7).

A *calendar to keep your schedule*–You need some kind of calendar to write down appointments, meetings, work schedule, or anything else that you make a commitment to attend. When you make a commitment to be somewhere, always write it down in your calendar so you don't forget. You can use a simple pocket calendar, or, if you want to get more sophisticated, you can use a PDA or computer software with a calendar.

HOW TO HAVE YOUR WEEKLY MEETING

Now that the tools are in place, set aside 30 minutes at the beginning of each week to plan out the entire week. During your "meeting with yourself" you should do the following things:

Clean out your inbox and your email inbox–Start by cleaning out all of the items you placed in your inbox through the week. Throw away what you don't need, then put the rest of your items into your files. When you need the items again, you will know right where to look! Also clean out the emails in your email inbox. Delete what you don't need, and file away the rest in your email folders for future reference.

Make a list of what needs to be done this week–Take a look at your master to-do list, and locate the items that need to be done this week by looking at the due date on each item. Then look for upcoming projects that you need to get started on now, even though they may not due for a while.

Write down this week's tasks in a place that is separate from your master to-do list–You can use your notebook to record this list each week, type them into a document on your computer, or whatever works for you. After you select this week's tasks, set aside your master to-do list. You will look at it again next week, but for now just concentrate on what needs to be done this week.

Use your calendar to make a schedule for the week–Now you are coming down the home stretch!

- *Set aside time to work on this week's tasks:* Look at your schedule for the week and decide what days and times will be best to work on your to-do list tasks. It's a good idea to actually enter this "to-do list time" onto your calendar so you will remember that time has been set aside.

- *Note any appointments or schedules you need to keep:* Check your calendar to see when you need to show up, and where. Be sure there are no conflicts and that you are clear on your schedule.

- *Don't fill up every minute of the week:* If every minute's full, there won't be time to relax, spend time with friends, and have fun. The point of time management isn't to fill up all of your time, it's simply to remember the basic things that need to be done.

Now that you have completed your weekly meeting, you know just what needs to be done this week and when you will work on it. You also have your schedule in mind so you know when to show up where. Use self-discipline to stick to the game plan, but if you need to make adjustments through the week, stay flexible enough to do so.

LIVE THE LEADERNETIC

1. What are the benefits of thinking a week at a time?

_____

_____

_____

2. What are the three basic tools of time management every leader should have in place?

_____

_____

_____

_____

3. What should you do each week during your weekly meeting with yourself?

_____

_____

_____

UNIT FOUR:
BECOMING A LEADER
IN STEP WITH GOD

9 BUILDING YOUR LIFE AND LEADERSHIP ON THE BIBLE

"There are more sure marks of authenticity in the Bible than in any profane history.... I have a fundamental belief in the Bible as the Word of God."
—Sir Isaac Netwton—

ORIGINAL TRUTH

Notes about this Leadernetic:

_____

_____

_____

_____

_____

_____

_____

_____

_____

Homer Simpson, in the "Homer Simpson vs Lisa and the Eighth Commandment" episode of *The Simpsons,* is faced with a moral dilemma. Homer gets hooked up to illegal cable, but Lisa (his daughter) learns at church that the eighth commandment says that stealing is wrong. So Lisa decides not to watch the illegal cable any longer and hopes that her family will follow. To display her opinion for all to see, she decides to protest outside the house on the day Homer is watching a big fight. Homer eventually has a dream about the Ten Commandments and, as a result, decides to unhook the illegal cable himself.

The Simpsons is just a TV show, but making moral decision is something that you face in real life. Every day you are faced with many "right or wrong" decisions with friends or colleagues, in school, or on the job. God's Word is the supreme source of truth. Like the sharp edge of a sword, it divides right from wrong with precision. As a leader, you have to make decisions based upon the truth of God's Word even if it doesn't line up with personal opinion, convenience, or mental reasoning.

Homer and Lisa both based their moral decision on the Bible, but they are unlike most Christian young adults in America. Less than one out of ten Christian young adults (7 percent to be exact) make moral decisions based on biblical principles. The remaining 93 percent make moral decisions about right and wrong based on what they feel is right for themselves and others at the time.[6]

THREE METHODS PEOPLE USE TO DETERMINE RIGHT FROM WRONG

What seems best at the time–Right and wrong can be determined by what makes sense for everyone involved. For example, if cheating on a test helps an athlete to be eligible to play ball and help the team, then it might be the right thing to do.

What feels right to you–Right and wrong can also be determined by how a person feels at a particular time. For example, if a person feels angry because CDs are priced too high, then it becomes acceptable to download music from the internet without paying for it.

God's Word–Right and wrong can also be determined by the standards that God has given us in His Word, regardless of how a person feels or what the situation might look like. For example, even if CDs cost $40 each (thankfully they don't!), it's always wrong to download illegally because that is stealing. Or even if the team loses and everybody is hurt, it's always wrong to cheat on the test because that is dishonesty.

GOD'S WORD IS THE RIGHT STANDARD OF TRUTH

The Creator makes the rules, not His creation—If you believe that God created the world, then it's illogical to make moral decisions based on your own feelings or opinions. That would be like the student telling the teacher how to grade the test, or the batter telling the umpire if the pitch was a strike or a ball. If God created the world, then He gets to call the shots. If you choose to call the shots, then you don't truly believe that God is the Creator of the universe, but you are instead setting yourself up as equal to God. You can't have it both ways—either you believe He is God or you don't.

The Bible has been proven true and supernatural—There are numerous angles to examine the authenticity of the Bible, and each one adds up to the same conclusion: The Bible's claim to be the Word of the Creator is true.

- *There is scientific proof:* Statements found in the Bible concerning astronomy (the study of the universe), paleontology (the study of dinosaurs), meteorology (the study of the earth), and anthropology (the study of humans) and other topics have been proven accurate. Many times scientific statements made in the Bible were contrary to beliefs held at the time but later were proven to be true.

- *There is prophetic proof:* Prophecy written in the Bible has turned out to be accurate. The statistical probability that all biblical prophecies come to pass is astronomical. Let's say you were to make a pile of quarters two feet deep and as wide as the state of Texas, then mark one quarter with a pen and drop it anywhere in the pile. Then you gave a stranger a chance to pick that marked quarter out of the pile on his first try. He would be facing the same statistical odds.

- *There is historical proof:* Many other well-accepted historical documents also support the historical claims of the Bible. There are many examples, but one of them is the book written in 115 AD called *The Annals* that verifies that a man named Christ lived on the earth, founded Christianity, and was crucified.

The Bible makes sense—Every command or standard that the Bible sets forth is designed to do two things: to protect and to provide. Although they may not feel good, they are there for our good, and if you think about them, they make sense. For example, God says not to have sex before marriage to protect you from disease, unwanted pregnancy, and heartache and to provide you with health, a stable family, and intimacy with your future spouse.

HOW TO BE A BIBLE-CENTERED LEADER

If you plan to use your leadership to shape the culture, you have to accept the Bible as the primary source of truth. It must become your personal standard for what is right and wrong. The following three suggestions will help you know how to do it:

Accept God's Word as truth, and don't be swayed–Many people will ridicule your belief in God's Word as absolute truth. You must have courage and stick to it, because according to Jesus, it's your job to defend what is right and stand against what is wrong. "Let me tell you why you are here," He says in Matthew 5:13. "You're here to be the salt-seasoning that brings out the God-flavors of this earth. If you lose your saltiness, how will people taste godliness? You've lost your usefulness and will end up in the garbage."

Establish a steady diet of God's Word–Find a way to be sure that you have a steady diet of God's Word coming into your mind. Follow God's challenge to Joshua: "Don't for a minute let this Book of the Revelation be out of mind. Ponder and meditate on it day and night, making sure you practice everything written in it. Then you'll get where you're going; then you'll succeed" (Joshua 1:8).

View the Bible as the starting point to wisdom and intellect–Accepting the Bible as absolute truth is not an exercise in stupidity—it's actually the true path to wisdom and intellect. "Start with God," Proverbs 1:7 says. "The first step in learning is bowing down to God; only fools thumb their noses at such wisdom and learning." Proverbs 2:20–22 makes a bold promise to those who make moral decision based on biblical principles: "Join in the company of good men and women, keep your feet on the tried and true paths. It's the men who walk straight who will settle this land, the women who walk with integrity who will last here. The corrupt will lose their lives; the dishonest will be gone for good."

LIVE THE LEADERNETIC

1. Explain the three different approaches a person can take when determing what is right and what is wrong.

   _____
   _____
   _____

2. What does the statement "The Creator makes the rules, not the creation" mean?

   _____
   _____
   _____
   _____

3. How can you become a Bible-centered leader?

   _____
   _____
   _____
   _____

10 BEING A LEADER IN STEP WITH GOD

"The question is not whether God still speaks. The question is whether we're still listening."
—Bob Reccord—

FOUR STEPS

Notes about this Leadernetic:

_____

_____

_____

_____

_____

_____

_____

_____

Trust God from the bottom of your heart; don't try to figure everything out on your own," Proverbs 3:5–6 tells us. "Listen for God's voice in everything you do, everywhere you go; He's the one who will keep you on track."

God-honoring leaders work with God to advance His purposes. God is at work on your campus, at your job, and in your community, and He wants to include you in His plans. By learning to hear God speak to you, you will be able to always remain in step with Him.

 William Wilberforce was an eighteenth-century politician in England. After his conversion to Christianity he considered becoming a pastor, but God spoke to him through his mentors that the right thing to do would be to stay in politics. He did, and soon after God led William to take up the cause of abolishing slavery in England. He first made a motion in the House of Commons in 1788, but his motion was voted down. He worked for eighteen years to see his bill passed. It wasn't until 1806 that the House of Commons voted to abolish slavery. Wilberforce knew all along that he was in step with God, and as a result, he left a permanent leadership legacy on the Western world.

God is not interested in hiding His plans from you. He wants to show you what He is doing! "I'm telling you this straight," Jesus says in John 5:19–20. "The Son can't independently do a thing, only what he sees the Father doing. What the Father does, the Son does. The Father loves the Son and includes Him on everything he is doing." Did you notice that Jesus said the Father wants to include you on what He is doing? If you are diligent to seek God's guidance for important decisions, He will tell you what you do. You can count on it.

You always need to hear from God, but there are several major areas in which you should always take special care when discerning what God is saying to you:

- Getting involved in a new area of leadership

- Responding to a difficult situation

- Choosing a college to attend

- Getting engaged and married

- Selecting or changing jobs/careers

BEING IN STEP WITH GOD MAKES YOUR LEADERSHIP COUNT

God is empowering you for a purpose–Although God has given you abilities, talents, and giftings, they must be empowered by the Holy Spirit to be truly usable in the hands of God. You should seek to understand how God has made you, how He wants to use you, and your unique purpose in life.

God is involving you in His work–God is at work around you all the time. He is working to accomplish His purposes in your school, community, and in your career field. You should seek to understand how God is working around you and how you can be a part of what He's doing.

God is expanding your character and ability–God is at work to develop your character. Remember, He is far more concerned with who you are rather than what you do, because if He can trust your character, He can also trust you with the big leadership jobs. If you stay in sync with Him, then you can count on Him doing this.

FOUR WAYS GOD OFTEN SPEAKS TO LEADERS

His Word–God's Word is true north when it comes to understanding His purposes. God has revealed a lot about His character and the way He works in His Word. The more you digest it, the more likely you are going to be thinking like God. And with a steady diet of God's Word active in your life, you will instinctively recognize anything that violates His precepts.

Trusted relationships–God designed you to live and lead in the context of relationships. You need both mentors and friends with whom you can share your thoughts, get advice, and gain perspective. It's remarkable how much a trusted friend will help you see and understand what God is doing when you sometimes can't see it yourself.

Your personal relationship with Him–There is nothing in the world that comes close to the awesome satisfaction of knowing your Creator! When Christ is a personal friend, you will naturally want to know what He wants because you know Him. Dive headfirst into a love relationship with God, and live for Him with complete passion.

Your situation–Being in step with God sometimes is a matter of opening your eyes and just looking around to see what He is doing. What new relationships are coming your way, and what do you think God is doing through them? What is working well, and why? What is not working well, and why? Use your common sense to observe how God might be working around you, and then get on board with Him.

HOW TO MAKE DECISIONS IN STEP WITH GOD

Evaluate your decision with God's Word–All decisions should begin by filtering the options through the truth in God's Word. It's the first tool to keep you in step with God and should also be the first way you evaluate decisions. Ask: "Does this opportunity or option resonate with the principles taught in God's Word?" If the answer is yes, then you can move on to the next step. But if the answer is no, then don't move ahead. Violating the principles in God's Word will always move you out of step with Him.

Get outside perspective–What do the people you you know and trust have to say? Talk with your parents, mentors, pastor, and friends. Ask for their input, and really listen to what they say. Also, consider what the situation reveals. If there are doors of opportunity opening up for you, then it's possible that God may be orchestrating the situation. Ask God to help you see it the way He sees it.

Listen to your own heart–What is your heart telling you? God will speak directly to you in times of important decision making. He will give you a gut feeling that something is right or wrong. It's not wise to base your decision solely on how you feel, but it does enter into the picture.

Make a decision with confidence–Once you take the time to evaluate a decision, make it. Don't drag your feet, and don't fear that you will somehow step away from God's plan. His will is not a tightrope, it's a circle. If you are asking the right questions and your heart is in step with God, then whatever you decide is going to keep you in step with God. Be confident and move ahead.

LIVE THE LEADERNETIC

1. How does being in step with God make your leadership count?

   _____

   _____

   _____

2. Describe the four ways that God often speaks to leaders.

   _____

   _____

   _____

   _____

3. What four steps are wise to follow when seeking God's guidance in a decision?

   _____

   _____

   _____

   _____

UNIT FIVE:
EMBRACING THE
INGREDIENTS TO
LEADERSHIP GROWTH

11 IDENTIFYING YOUR LEADERSHIP STRENGTHS

"I can't believe that God put us on the earth to be ordinary."
—Lou Holtz—

DIAMOND IN THE ROUGH

Notes about this Leadernetic:

_____

_____

_____

_____

_____

_____

_____

_____

God has placed within you the ability to lead in a way that is completely unique to you. Make no mistake about it—He has placed the potential within you. Consider what David has to say about you in Psalm 139:

"Oh yes, you shaped me first inside, then out; you formed me in my mother's womb. I thank you, High God—you're breathtaking! Body and soul, I am marvelously made! I worship in adoration—what a creation! You know me inside and out, you know every bone in my body; you know exactly how I was made, bit by bit, how I was sculpted from nothing into something. Like an open book, you watched me grow from conception to birth; all the stages of my life were spread out before you, the days of my life all prepared before I'd even lived one day" (Psalm 139:13-16).

But just because God has placed within you the ability to lead doesn't mean you are ready to go out and do it! You must first understand the way God has made you, and then you must develop those God-given abilities. Your hard work—along with a dependency on God—will turn your leadership potential into leadership ability.

LEADER PROFILE John Baker, an eighteen-year-old senior at Hayesville High School in North Carolina, wanted to do something to raise money to provide scholarships for graduating seniors. But how would a high-school student find the money to fund a scholarship? For John that was an easy answer. He looked within at the two things he loved the most: writing and football. John wrote and published a book about the history of football at Hayesville High School. And the town bought the books like wildfire—enough that John was able to sock away $14,000 to get his scholarship fund started. John had within him the talents to do what set out to do.[7] He had the ability to communicate well, and he was good at organizing people. He combined those abilities with his passion for sports and the need for scholarships to make quite a contribution as a leader.

Like John, God has given you the abilities to take initiative to make a difference in your areas of passion. The only question is this: Will you be committed enough to develop that God-given potential?

YOUR GOD-GIVEN ABILITIES FALL INTO THREE CATEGORIES

The best way to begin to understand how God has "wired" you to lead is to think of your abilities in three separate, but equally important, categories.

Natural strengths–A strength (sometimes also called a talent) is an attitude or ability that you were born with. Nobody had to teach you these things. You can use your strengths productively because they come naturally to you. Through years of research, the Gallup Organization has identified thirty-four overall possible strengths, of which you probably have about five.[8] A few examples of Gallup's strengths are:

- *Achiever*: Someone who is has a lot of stamina and loves to work hard

- *Activator*: Someone who can quickly turn thoughts into action

- *Analytical*: Someone who wants to know how things work

- *Arranger*: Someone who is great at organizing

- *Communication*: Someone who can easily put their thoughts into words

- *Empathy*: Someone who can sense the feelings of others

- *Futuristic*: Someone who is inspired by the future and what could be

- *Learner*: Someone who wants to learn and continually improve

- *Relator*: Someone who is strong in building relationships

- *Self-assurance*: Someone who is naturally very confident in themselves

Spiritual gifts–When you became a follower of Christ, He placed within you certain abilities that you need to have in order to fulfill His purpose for your life. There are many spiritual gifts listed in the Bible, and it's likely that you have a mixture of two or three of these spiritual gifts. Some examples of spiritual gifts are:

- *Pastoring*: Caring for the spiritual growth of others

- *Discernment*: The ability to understand beyond what is seen

- *Faith*: The ability to believe for great miracles to happen

- *Giving*: The ability to give to others with great generosity

- *Administration*: The ability to organize and create structure

There are many more gifts listed in the Bible. Depending on your theological orientation, there may be anywhere from nine to several dozen spiritual gifts.

Personality–Your personality gives you a unique way of interacting with other people and situations around you. Although some personalities are more gregarious and outgoing, you can be a leader regardless of what kind of personality you have. There are numerous ways to understand your personality, but some examples are:

- Some people draw energy from being around a lot of people; others draw energy from being alone or with a smaller group.

- Some people focus on what they perceive with the five senses; others focus more on what they see in more abstract patterns.

- Some people make decisions based more on facts and information; others make decisions based more on what will make others happy.

- Some people like to be decisive and plan out the details; others like to keep all their options open and just "go with the flow."

In the early stages of your leadership journey, it's very helpful to learn about yourself by examining these three areas of your "leadership wiring." And throughout your lifetime, as your experience and maturity grow, you will learn more about how God has enabled you to lead.

DEVELOPING YOUR GOD-GIVEN ABILITIES WILL EXPAND YOUR INFLUENCE

Knowing and understanding your God-given abilities will naturally result in you being a stronger leader. There are three reasons this is true:

You will understand how and where you should be leading–When you understand how God made you, it will become easier for you to match your abilities with various opportunities on your campus, in your community, and within your church. You will also be able to make educational and career choices based on what you know God has wired you to do.

You will begin to understand your purpose in life–If God has a special purpose for your life (which He does!), and if God created you with very special and unique abilities (which He did!) then the two of them will match up with each other. Your God-given "wiring" is like a small snapshot of why He placed you on the earth. Discover how you were made, and you will understand more about why God placed you on the earth.

You will be more effective in the projects and roles you take on–If you are serving in a leadership role that matches your abilities, then if you work hard to improve your natural abilities, it only makes sense that you will be more effective as a leader. You will enjoy what you do, you will do a good job, and God gets the glory for it!

HOW TO DEVELOP YOUR GOD-GIVEN ABILITIES

So, how do you actually go about developing your God-given abilities? Allow me to give you three suggestions:

Use assessment tools to learn about yourself–Here are three possible assessment tools that you can use to learn more about how God created you. These tools have each been developed through years of research and are each very effective.

- *Strengths Assessment.* Visit www.strengthsquest.org to take an assessment designed specifically for you to understand your natural strengths.

- *Spiritual Gifts Assessment.* Talk to a pastor at your church about taking a spiritual gifts assessment.

- *Personality Assessment.* Talk to your school counselor about taking a personality assessment—there are many possible options.

Ask for perspective from others–Ask others to help you gain perspective on what you are good at doing and also how to find more specific leadership roles that are a match with where you should be leading. It's very helpful to discuss the results of your assessments with someone who knows you well and can help you put what you learn into use.

Create a plan to develop your abilities–When you discover how God has made you, begin to consider what you can do to take the "raw materials" and refine them into what God designed them to be. Remember, your gifts are like a diamond in the rough. Not only do you have to put some energy into identifying them, you also have to work hard to develop them to their highest potential.

LIVE THE LEADERNETIC

1. What are the three categories that you can use to understand how God has "wired" you as a leader?

   _____

   _____

   _____

2. Why does developing your God-given abilities expand your influence?

   _____

   _____

   _____

   _____

3. What are three steps you can take to develop your God-given abilities?

   _____

   _____

   _____

12 DEVELOPING A PERSONAL GROWTH PLAN

"It's what you learn after you know it all that counts."
—John Woode

SUPERSIZED DREAMS

Notes about this Leadernetic:

_____

_____

_____

_____

_____

_____

_____

_____

_____

I n Luke 2:52, the Bible says, "Jesus grew in wisdom and stature and in favor with God and men" (NIV). When most of us think about personal growth, our attention is often drawn to the areas of life that we struggle in. Weaknesses, not strengths, are typically our focus. And because of that focus, it can be difficult for us to imagine Jesus as our model for personal growth. After all, why would the Son of God need to grow? Isn't He perfect already?

While Jesus is perfect, the Bible is still clear that personal growth was a priority in His life. And Luke 2:52 describes four areas in which his growth was focused—wisdom (mentally), stature (physically), favor with God (spiritually), and favor with men (socially). Was Jesus weak in these areas and therefore found a need for concentrated growth? I don't think so. I believe Jesus was strong in all of these areas. But his growth built on his strengths. And the result was remarkable. John 17:4 says, "I have brought you glory on earth by completing the work you gave me to do"(NIV). Jesus' commitment to personal growth enabled him to fulfill the purpose for which the Father had sent him.

The same should be true for us today. Our growth should not only focus on the weaknesses that could ultimately derail us, but it should also build on our strengths. Why? Because each of us will make our greatest impact in the world through our strengths. And growing our strengths to their full potential will enable us to reach the dreams God has planted within us.

 Born on December 30, 1975, in Cypress, California, Eldrick grew up with one passion—golf. His father, a retired U.S. Army Lieutenant Colonel, taught Eldrick the sport at a very young age. He imitated his father's swing, and by age 2 shot a 48 on a nine-hole Navy course. As a teenager, Eldrick attended Western High School in Cypress, California. He continued to hone his skills on the course and soon set records that boggled the mind. At age 15 he became the youngest U.S. Junior Amateur Champion in the history of golf. And in 1994, at the age of 18, he won the U.S. Amateur Championship. But Eldrick wasn't content. He practiced long and hard and developed an immense focus. His goal: to be the best golfer in the world! After graduating from high school, he attended Stanford University on a golf scholarship. He wasn't treated any differently than the rest of the team and got his initiation carrying golf bags during road trips.

Eldrick left Stanford to go pro, and in 1997, at the age of 21, he took home the Masters, becoming the youngest winner in history. The wins rolled into Eldrick's life, followed by endorsement deals from Nike and

Titleist totaling $60 million. It was like a machine emerged over the horizon of golf that never slowed down. World, meet Eldrick "Tiger" Woods.

Named after a friend of his father's in the Vietnam War, Tiger had a tenacious obsession with his personal growth as a golfer. Gary Player once said, "The average man, he looks at a man like Tiger Woods and says, 'Gee, all he does is play golf and make this money.' That is not true. It took years and years of sacrifice, and it's a massive sacrifice to become a world champion."[9] In 1998, after an impressive winning record, Tiger refused to get complacent. He began working on a new swing, aiming to become even better. It cost him an 11-tournament losing streak, but he was determined to grow into the best golfer in the world. And his effort paid off. In 2000, he won the U.S. Open, the British Open, and the PGA Championship. Then he won the Masters, sweeping all four major titles. He was ranked the number one golfer in the world, and in 2005, Tiger's career earnings passed $61 million.

GROWING TOWARD YOUR DREAMS

Tiger Woods is a remarkable example of personal growth. And when you look at his life, you can see his commitment to growth exemplified in several areas. First, his growth builds on his strengths and passion for golf. Second, his growth has been enhanced by the input of golf coaches such as Butch Harmon and Hank Haney. And third, his growth is marked by a tremendous amount of discipline.

Personal growth takes time, energy, and discipline. It isn't something that comes naturally. In fact, you've probably heard it said that the only thing that's natural is dying. Growing, on the other hand, requires change, and change is sometimes difficult. But change is also the only way you'll reach your dreams.

In your school there is no shortage of students who have a dream for the future. And there's no doubt that many of these dreams are incredibly significant. But it's one thing to have a dream and something entirely different to reach your dream. And the only way to reach your dream is grow from the person you are today into the person you need to become so that your dream can actually come true.

It's kind of like wearing an oversized set of clothes. When you were younger you might have slipped on your dad's shoes or put on an oversized set of clothes that belonged to an older brother or sister. Wearing those clothes and walking in those shoes was difficult, and you were probably somewhat clumsy as you attempted to walk or run. But the problem wasn't the clothes—you just needed to grow into them.

The same is true of reaching your dreams. Having big dreams isn't the problem. In fact, it's a good thing to dream big. But the only way to make those dreams become a reality is to grow into them. In other words, you have to become the person that is able to reach those dreams. If you could reach them as the person you are today, those dreams would no longer be dreams—they'd be reality. In the same way Jesus grew toward the fulfillment of His purpose, you have to grow toward the fulfillment of your dreams. And while Tiger Woods once dreamed of being a golf champion, he didn't stop at dreaming. He grew into a golf champion.

HOW TO DEVELOP A GROWTH PLAN

If reaching your dreams requires growth, then you have to develop an intentional plan to grow. Again, growth doesn't happen by accident. It requires a well-developed plan. And the best way to develop a good personal growth plan is to answer four important questions:

In what areas do you want to grow? Growth begins by determining in which areas of your life you desire to grow. While some areas might address a weakness such as character issues, attitude problems, poor habits, or undisciplined behavior, your growth should also focus on your strengths. Look at your abilities, skills, and passions to determine which of these you desire to grow to an entirely new level. Even further, identify the areas in which you must grow in order to reach your dreams. If you have a leadership role on campus or in your community, you might determine to grow your skills in that particular role. Or you may decide to focus on growing important relationships with family, friends, or with God.

How do you plan to grow? Determining in what areas you want to grow isn't enough. You must have a plan that maps out how you will grow. This is where many people drop the ball. It's like many New Year's resolutions. How many people have you known who made a New Year's resolution only to blow it before the end of January? Was the problem the resolution? Probably not! The problem is a failure to develop a well-thought-out plan to help them reach the resolution. Once you identify the areas where you desire to grow, you must determine what action steps, tools, and ideas will help you grow. In other words, do you need to read a book, enroll in a class, pursue a mentor, plan a project, practice a skill, purchase a resource, attend a conference, or get experience to help you grow?

Who will help you grow? Most of us aren't good enough to grow by ourselves. We need people to come alongside of us to help us accelerate our growth process. And the best people to help us grow are mentors, coaches, and accountability partners. Anybody could serve as a mentor or coach, including a parent, teacher, pastor, mature friend, business leader, or somebody with a specific set of skills or habits you desire to cultivate. Having a mentor or coach enables you to grow by accessing the insight and wisdom of somebody who has more life experience than you. Accountability partners can also be extremely beneficial. They can help you grow by holding you accountable to your growth plan and asking you questions to ensure you're doing what you set out to accomplish.

When and how will you evaluate progress? Finally, every growth goal needs to be evaluated. In other words, if you determine to grow in your ability to manage your time, develop a specific plan to help, and find a leader to mentor you in time management skills, eventually you'll need to evaluate whether or not you're making progress. This evaluation process might happen once per month or even once every three months. The key is to designate a time to evaluate whether you're actually growing and determine if you need to make any adjustments to your growth plan. By evaluating progress throughout the year, you'll be much more likely to reach your growth goals.

LIVE THE LEADERNETIC

1. How does personal growth influence your ability to reach your dreams?

   _____
   _____
   _____

2. Why should your growth plan not only address liabilities in your life but also build on your strengths?

   _____
   _____
   _____
   _____

3. What are the four questions you should answer when developing a personal growth plan?

   _____
   _____
   _____

13 FINDING A LEADERSHIP COACH

"I can go farther and faster with someone coaching me than I can on my own."
—Andy Stanley—

THE COACH

Notes about this Leadernetic:

_____

_____

_____

_____

_____

_____

_____

_____

_____

None of us could ever imagine a Super Bowl championship football team without an equally talented team of coaches. The coaches have the ability to take a team player's skills to an entirely new level. They have insight into what it takes to move from being a group of individuals with great talent to a unified team of champions with the ability to be the best in the league. Coaches are often the difference-maker in helping players maximize their efforts and catapult their performance to the top of their game.

But coaching was never meant to be limited to the sports arena. In the same way a football player can have a coach, any student desiring to grow their leadership skills can also have a coach. While the focus of the coaching may be different, the idea of having a coach is the same.

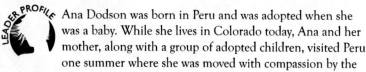 Ana Dodson was born in Peru and was adopted when she was a baby. While she lives in Colorado today, Ana and her mother, along with a group of adopted children, visited Peru one summer where she was moved with compassion by the immense need among orphans. While in Cusco, Peru, Ana visited an orphanage where she encountered thirty abused and abandoned girls. Ana said, "When I returned to Colorado, I could not forget the faces of the girls, and the way they hugged me and appreciated my visit."

At the age of 13, Ana decided to do something to make a difference. She approached her parents and asked if they would help her form a nonprofit organization called "Peruvian Hearts." Peruvian Hearts provides orphans with school supplies, vitamins, books, toiletries, clothing, medicine, quilts, backpacks, and toys. And they have contributed funds to help purchase firewood and food for the orphanage in Cusco, Peru. In one year, Ana collected nearly $15,000 worth of donations, and she created a DVD to spread the word about Peruvian Hearts. Ana's fundraising efforts have moved beyond Colorado to Illinois, Maryland, Massachusetts, Vermont, and Wisconsin. She recently commented, "My life has been filled with gifts of love and friendship and the opportunity to have a wonderful education... I want the same for the girls in Peru."[10]

Ana is a young leader who's using her influence to meet needs and solve problems. But I want you to notice an important ingredient in her success. When the dream was born to make a difference in the lives of orphans, Ana didn't try to go it alone. She sought guidance by asking a "coach" for help in forming a nonprofit organization. She was willing to admit what she didn't know and pursued a coach that could give her the advice and help she needed. In this case, the coach was her parents.

WHAT IS A COACH & WHY DO I NEED ONE?

In his book, *The Next Generation Leader,* author and pastor Andy Stanley identifies a coach as someone who does three things: observes, instructs, and inspires. A good coach begins by observing the individual or the team he or she is coaching. If you play sports you know this to be true. Your coach watches you play and looks for what you're doing right and what you're doing wrong. But your coach won't stop there. He then instructs you on how to do things better. He gives you tips, pointers, and insight on how to sharpen your skills and improve your performance. And when you hit the field ready to play the game, your coach is there as a motivator, inspiring you to give your best.

In the same way a sports coach observes, instructs, and inspires, a coach for any other area of life will do the same. For example, if you want to grow in your ability to effectively plan a project, then a good coach would be someone who has great organizational skills and the ability to think and plan strategically. If you found an adult with these skills and then asked them to coach you, they might begin by giving you a few pointers. But invariably they're going to watch your performance along the way. They'll be looking at what you do right and what you can do better. After watching you, they'll give you some practical instruction on how to improve. And because they believe in you, they'll encourage you and inspire you to keep at it. In a sense, they'll be like a cheerleader as you grow your planning skills.

This same coaching is available for any area of life where you want to grow. Whether it's sports, music, relationships, team-building, time management, speaking skills, or any number of interests, there are countless men and women who are qualified to serve as coaches in your life.

HOW DO I FIND A COACH?

The idea of coaching isn't new. In fact, Jesus modeled it for us in His relationship with the disciples. Mark 3:13–15 says, "Jesus went up on a mountainside and called to him those he wanted, and they came to him. He appointed twelve—designating them apostles—*that they might be with him and that he might send them out* to preach and to have authority to drive out demons"(NIV; emphasis mine). Jesus was willing to invest time and energy into growing His disciples and releasing them to make a difference in the world. Today you need a coach in your life as well—perhaps more than one. So what does it take to find and benefit from a coaching relationship? Consider three things:

Determine what kind of coach you need–You make this determination by first understanding what your dreams are and in which areas of your life you want to grow. If you don't know your dreams or your growth goals, you won't know what to look for in a coach. It only makes sense to get a coach that is strong in the areas you desire to grow.

Make a list of potential coaches–Coaches may be parents, pastors, youth leaders, teachers, business men/women, an older sibling, or a grandparent. The list could be endless. The key is to look for the right person... someone who can truly help you grow in the areas of life you've identified.

Ask someone to help you grow–The term coaching might scare some people away. Instead of asking someone to coach you, consider asking them to evaluate a particular area of your life and to help you take steps to grow in those areas. Then, when they give you instruction or advice, be willing to do what they say. If you're not teachable, it's going to be difficult to benefit from a coach.

Let me give you one final piece of advice. Coaching is not something reserved for the younger years of life; it's something we should embrace throughout our lifetime so we can continually become everything God has called us to be. When we experience a measure of success it can be tempting to stop growing and stop pursuing coaching relationships. But you can't afford to make that mistake. The coaching was a key ingredient to your success. And your willingness to maintain a learning attitude will allow you to benefit from coaching long into the future. As Andy Stanley says, "In the early years of your career *what you learn is far more important that what you earn.* In most cases, what you learn early on will determine what you earn later on." And that learning attitude also applies to your journey as a student–what you learn today has a direct bearing on your leadership ability tomorrow.

LIVE THE LEADERNETIC

1. What are the three roles of a coach, and why should you pursue coaching relationships?

   _____

   _____

   _____

2. How did Jesus serve as a coach to His disciples?

   _____

   _____

   _____

   _____

3. What are the three keys to finding a coach?

   _____

   _____

   _____

   _____

UNIT SIX:
USING YOUR LEADERSHIP TO MAKE A DIFFERENCE

14 BEING A CULTURE-SHAPING LEADER

"Every Christian must consciously
commit to impacting the culture. To do
that requires influence."
—**Hugh Hewitt**—

MAKING WAVES

Notes about this Leadernetic:

_____

_____

_____

_____

_____

_____

_____

_____

The idea of leadership can bring a wide variety of things to mind. Some people think of positions or titles, others think of famous people, and still others envision leadership qualities such as character, vision, or skills. But we want to challenge you to think about leadership from a larger perspective. Rather than limiting your ideas to who a leader is or how a leader leads, think for a moment about what a leader accomplishes. In other words, what are the outcomes or results of a leader's influence? At the end of the day, is a leader simply more popular, better at a leadership skill, or having acquired more power? Or is there something more?

Envision for a moment more than what kind of leader you want to be or how you could go about influencing others. Think about the outcomes. In other words, what do you want to be the result of your leadership? If your leadership is going to be truly significant, it must move beyond a self-centered focus to a realization that the greatest leaders are those who create positive and healthy change in the world around them. And to have this kind of influence will require that we move beyond our Christian bubble and endeavor to become a culture-shaping leader.

WHAT IS A CULTURE-SHAPING LEADER?

A culture-shaping leader is someone that uses their influence to help people and change culture. Using their God-given abilities, skills, and gifts, these leaders endeavor to:

- Gain influence in a way that honors God
- Meet needs, solve problems, and help people
- Stand up for what's right
- Share Christ
- Walk in step with God

And as leaders do these five things, they will influence the culture in which we live by being the salt of the earth and the light of the world.

The Bible says in Matthew 5:13–16, "You are the salt of the earth. But if the salt loses its saltiness, how can it be made salty again? It is no longer good for anything, except to be thrown out and trampled by men. You are the light of the world. A city on a hill cannot be hidden. Neither do people light a lamp and put it under a bowl. Instead they put it on its stand, and it gives light to everyone in the house. In the same way, let your light shine before men, that they may see your good deeds and praise your Father in heaven" (NIV).

Salt has two primary functions—to preserve and to flavor. When Jesus called us to be the salt of the earth, he was calling us to preserve and add flavor to our world. By standing up for what's right we preserve our world from moral decay. And by meeting needs, solving problems, and helping people we add flavor to our world making life better for others. Jesus also declared, "You are the light of the world." By sharing the hope of Christ with others and allowing our behavior and deeds to point people to Him, we are being light into a dark world. And this entire process of being salt and light was never meant to be done alone. It's a partnership with God and what He desires to accomplish in and through us.

We will examine courageous decision-making (salt) and sharing Christ (light) in the next two chapters, but for now I want you to grasp one very important ingredient in this process. If we are going to become culture-shaping leaders, it will require us to move beyond our Christian bubble and gain influence in our community and in society at large.

SUBMARINE, HOVERCRAFT, OR BATTLESHIP?

Many Christians today allow their life and leadership to swing to one of two extremes. At one extreme they are like a submarine. Submarines immerse themselves in the water, yet have very little influence on it. In the same way, some people who claim to follow Christ immerse themselves in the world, yet demonstrate little positive influence. Rather than creating change in the culture, they actually become like the culture. As Jack Hayford once said, "I can't change the world if the world has changed me."

At the other end of the spectrum, some Christians have a knee-jerk reaction to the world. Rather than using their influence to meet needs, solve problems, and help people in society, they restrict their life and leadership to a Christian bubble. All of their time is spent with other Christians; therefore, they have little influence on the needs and problems of the world. These Christians are more like a hovercraft. While they can be commended for their life of purity and holiness, they have failed to make any difference in their community. They hover above the world, yet rarely help or lead those within it.

Between these two extremes is a third option—to become a battleship. Submarines and hovercraft have one thing in common—they have little effect upon the world. But a battleship slices through the water and its influence can be felt. It doesn't sink below the water, acting no different than those who don't know Christ. And it doesn't hover above the water unwilling to influence our culture. Instead, a follower of Christ who acts and lives like a battleship is willing to uphold a biblical and God-honoring lifestyle while at the same time creating change in our culture. They don't run from the world creating their own "Christian culture," but rather gain influence in the world where they can be the salt of the earth and the light of the world. Throughout this entire process they seek to be in step with God and His work in and through their lives.

MORE ON WHAT JESUS SAID

Perhaps you want to know more about what Jesus' perspective on culture-shaping leadership is. The truth is, He inspired the entire idea. In addition to his challenge in Matthew 5, Jesus prayed that his disciples would become culture-shapers. John 17 records Jesus' prayer for his disciples. In verses 15–19, Jesus prays, "My prayer is not that you take them out of the world but that you protect them from the evil one. They are not of the world, even as I am not of it. Sanctify them by the truth; your word is truth. As you sent me into the world, I have sent them into the world. For them I sanctify myself, that they too may be truly sanctified" (NIV).

Jesus prayed two things for his disciples in these verses. First, he prayed that they would be sanctified. You may be wondering what in the world it means to be sanctified. The word *sanctified* means "to be set apart." Jesus was praying that the behavior, values, and belief system of his disciples would be set apart from the worlds. He understood that you have to be different before you can make a difference. But his prayer didn't stop there. Jesus made two unique statements in his prayer. He said, "My prayer is not that you take them out of the world" *and* "As you sent me into the world, I have sent them into the world." What an incredible balance. Jesus prayed that his disciples would be "sanctified" and "sent." He wanted them to be set apart in their lifestyle but did not want them to withdraw from the world. They were to live in the world where their faith could make a difference.

 As a young child, Samuel Robison was a patient at Huntsville Hospital in Huntsville, Alabama. While receiving pediatric care at the hospital, Samuel noticed that many of the toys were "outdated and didn't work very well." After his stay at the hospital, Samuel cleaned out his toybox at home and donated video-game systems and toys. This started a journey in Samuel's life to help raise money for the pediatric unit of the hospital.

As a seventh-grader at Holy Spirit Regional School in Huntsville, Samuel started a fundraising drive called "Pocket Change for Peds" to benefit pediatric patients. With the help of a friend, Samuel placed piggybanks in eighteen classrooms at their school and asked students to bring pocket change from home. Over the course of the year they raised over $2,500 to purchase toys for Huntsville Hospital.

Today Samuel has stretched his vision and is endeavoring to raise $75,000 to help build a rooftop garden and playground at the hospital. He spent last summer contacting schools through Madison County, developed brochures and presentations about the project, distributed fliers, and contacted businesses and politicians for support. So far he has raised $40,000. Samuel said, "I just want to help other kids, and hope that I can help make a difference in their lives."[11]

Samuel has chosen to use his influence as a battleship. He hasn't confined his leadership to Christians alone but has chosen to be a leader in his community as well. Samuel is making waves. And that's what culture-shaping leaders do.

LIVE THE LEADERNETIC

1. What is a culture-shaping leader, and what does a culture-shaping leader do?

   _____

   _____

   _____

2. What three types of Christians are there today, and which one are you?

   _____

   _____

   _____

3. How does Jesus challenge us to become a culture-shaping leader?

   _____

   _____

   _____

   _____

15 MAKING COURAGEOUS LEADERSHIP DECISIONS

"You gain courage, strength, and confidence by every experience in which you really stop to look fear in the face."
—**Eleanor Roosevelt**—

PLAY BOTH WAYS

Notes about this Leadernetic:

_____

_____

_____

_____

_____

_____

_____

_____

_____

The story of David and Goliath has been rehearsed hundreds of times in churches around the world. You might even get a mental image of the first time you heard the story as a kid in Sunday school. But behind the simplicity of perhaps the most popular Bible story you've ever read are some incredible lessons on courage. Consider this:

Courage is not the absence of fear–In fact, when you read 1 Samuel 17:24, David's initial response to Goliath was the same as the Israelites–he ran in fear. David was scared of this giant that towered over the armies at over nine feet tall. Yet in the middle of his fear he found courage to act.

Courage opens the door of opportunity–As David mingled among the Israelite army, he quickly discovered that the person who killed Goliath would receive three things: great wealth, marriage to the king's daughter, and exemption from taxes. What an incredible opportunity! But it was an opportunity that waited on the other side of courage. And the same is true today. Sometimes our greatest opportunities await us if we'll simply have the courage to act in the face of fear.

Courage is necessary to solve problems–Goliath was a problem to the Israelites, and day after day they were reminded of the problem by his defiant speech. But through an act of courage, David tackled the problem head-on. The Bible says that he ran to the battle to meet him. Whereas he once ran from the problem, now David was courageously facing the problem.

Courage can change the momentum of your life–With a stone David killed Goliath as it sank into his forehead. And once David cut off Goliath's head, something amazing happened–the momentum shifted. First Samuel 17:51 says, "When the Philistines saw that their hero was dead, they turned and ran" (NIV). David's single act of courage changed the momentum for an entire nation. Because he looked fear in the face and acted boldly, a great victory was won.

 At the age of 17, Devin Cohen from Briarcliff High School in New York caught a vision to make a difference in the lives of young cancer patients. Devin was volunteering as a play partner with children undergoing cancer treatments when he noticed that many of the toys in the hospital were old and outdated. Many people see needs like this but do nothing about them. Devin, however, made a courageous decision to act on the need before him. He solicited local merchants for donations so he could purchase new toys for children in 26 hospitals across the country. Devin said, "Ultimately, it became clear to me that these sick children, many of whom had families that were financially devastated because of their child's disease, needed many things to improve their quality of life and remind them that inside their sick bodies lived a normal child."

As Devin's awareness of the need increased, he made yet another courageous decision. Rather than limiting his contacts to local businesses, he contacted national corporations to enlist their support. Many corporations responded by donating toys, video games, movies, and books. And Devin has arranged for pediatric units to receive donated electronic equipment, furniture, and other needed items. But he didn't stop there. Devin partnered with Gap to provide back-to-school clothes for kids with cancer, supplied AT&T phone cards to hospitalized children, arranged makeovers and beauty products for teenage girls with cancer, and secured tickets to sporting events and Broadway shows for sick kids. In all, Devin has obtained more than $150,000 worth of donated goods for young cancer patients. And because of his willingness to courageously act by meeting the needs of cancer patients, Devin has founded a teen committee to help raise money for a new children's hospital at Westchester Medical Center.[12]

PLAYING OFFENSE AND DEFENSE

What makes Devin's story so powerful isn't that he saw a need, but that he chose to do something about it. And that's what makes him a leader. His courage to act on a need has catapulted his influence. Ultimately Devin learned the power of playing offense with his decisions. And equally important to playing offense is a willingness to play defense.

Play offense with your decisions–Anytime a football team has the ball, they're playing offense. Their goal is to move the ball down the field and ultimately score a touchdown. So how does a leader play offense with his or her decisions? In other words, what does a touchdown look like for a leader? Leaders play offense when they decide to meet a need, solve a problem, or help people. That's when they score. That's exactly what David did when he fought Goliath. And it's exactly what Devin Cohen did when he helped young cancer patients.

Play defense with your decisions–A football team plays defense when they don't have the ball. In other words, they're holding the line, doing their best to prevent a touchdown by the other team. And when leaders play defense with their decisions, they're choosing to stand up for what's morally right. Rather than backing down from pressure to do something that's morally wrong, they hold the line and stand up for what's right. By playing defense, leaders prevent unbiblical views from prevailing in their area of influence.

Here's what I want you to grasp—as a leader, you must play *both* offense and defense. You've got to play both ways. And doing so takes courage. It isn't easy acting on the needs and problems around you. It's not always easy seeing people from God's perspective and then choosing to help them. And it's almost never convenient standing up for what's right. That's why it takes courage. Courage is needed to see a need and act on it and to take a stand for truth. Even in the midst of fear, courageous leaders play both ways. And when you play both ways, you will experience what David did—new opportunities, the solving of problems, and a shift in momentum.

LIVE THE LEADERNETIC

1. What lessons on courage can we learn from the life of David?

_____

_____

_____

2. What does it mean to play offense with your decisions?

_____

_____

_____

_____

3. What does it mean to play defense with your decisions?

_____

_____

_____

_____

16 SHARING CHRIST WITH OTHERS

"The Gospel, in its essence, is a message of hope to a world full of despair."
—Erwin McManus—

THE LIGHT OF LEADERSHIP

Notes about this Leadernetic:

_____

_____

_____

_____

_____

_____

_____

_____

_____

Jesus came to bring a message of good news to the lost. "God's spirit is upon me," He said in Luke 4:18–19. "He's chosen me to preach the Message of good news to the poor, sent me to announce pardon to prisoners and recovery of sight to the blind, to set the burdened and battered free, to announce 'This is God's year to act!'"

But we have a problem. According to research, the top four ways the average 16- to 29-year-old American describes Christians are:

- anti-homosexual (91% say this is true)

- judgmental (87%)

- hypocritical (85%)

- insensitive to others (70%)[13]

If these findings are true, much of our society has a mixed-up view of Christians. This presents a profound responsibility and opportunity for you as a leader to use your influence to reshape the way others view Christ and the hope that He can give.

 Jason Gonzolez plays baseball for the best team in Utah. At Taylorsville High School where the baseball team goes to state every year, the baseball players have the highest status of all the athletes, and Jason is one of the best on the team. Jason works very hard to build friendships with the other guys on the team, even when they screw up or they get themselves in trouble. Jason is a true friend, and people look up to Jason because of it. He is able to use his influence to present a true image of Christ and the hope He brings.[14]

How can you as a leader go about presenting a true image of Christ to those around you, just as Jason has done in his area of leadership? Let's begin by understanding why many don't view Christ in a positive way.

UNDERSTAND WHY MANY PEOPLE DON'T VIEW CHRISTIANS IN A POSITIVE WAY

Christians tend to put conditions on our friendships with those who don't know Christ—We will be friends with unbelievers just so we can share Christ with them. And if they don't embrace our views or become a Christian, there's a certain point that we let the relationship go away.

The established church in Jesus' day (the Pharisees) also had the same tendency. Once they even got publicly angry at Jesus because He was spending so much time with nonbelievers (Mark 2:16–17). They asked him, "What kind of example is this, acting cozy with the riff-raff?" Jesus shot back, "Who needs a doctor: the healthy or the sick? I'm here inviting the sin-sick, not the spiritually fit." The religious were elitist, but Jesus was loving and inclusive. Which are you?

Christians tend to spend a lot of time pointing out problems and evils—We spend a lot of time pointing out the problems and too little time solving those problems and showing people hope in Christ. Once Jesus got into a verbal scuffle with some religious folks when they were being judgmental of a man because of the sin in his life (John 9:39). Jesus said to them, "I came into the world to bring everything into the clear light of day... so that people who have never seen will see.... " Jesus was far more concerned with giving people a reason to hope than He was concerned with pointing out their shortcomings.

HOW TO REPRESENT CHRIST IN A LOVING WAY

Represent Christ as He would if He were walking in your shoes—If Christ were on the earth today, the average 16- to 29-year old would say:

- He asks me to follow Him with total abandon, but will still be my friend if I don't.
- He values me and what I believe while He is holding firm to truth.
- He cares about me; I mean really cares a lot.
- He wants me to find hope and meaning through a relationship with Him.

Build genuine friendships with those in your place of leadership—It's important to pursue leadership roles that give you the opportunity to influence those who don't know Christ. And as you do, build genuine friendships with nonbelievers. Don't get to know them so you can share Christ. Get to know them because you like them and want to be their friend.

Focus more on the hope of Christ than on pointing out what's wrong in the lives of others around you—Don't focus on the shortcomings you see in the lives of those around you. Instead, focus on allowing others to see the light of Christ in your life. It will speak for itself and will be far more likely to transform others than if you focus on what is wrong.

Along the same lines, spend more time celebrating what is good in society than highlighting what is evil. Even better, be the one who creates things that are positive in the midst of our society's problems.

Have meaningful conversations with your friends—Before you can share Christ with others, they have to know you as a person. Get to know others beyond surface relationships. Allow them to know your struggles, joys, and dreams. Before others can see how Christ relates to them, they have to relate to you. When they see themselves in your life and see that Christ has changed you then they will understand how He relates to their life as well.

Openly and plainly explain your faith in Christ—Talk openly about your faith in Christ. Think of it naturally, no different than discussing your favorite sports team or a hobby but with the passion of something that has changed your life! When others see that you are comfortable with your faith and that it's a part of your everyday life, they will want to know Christ as well.

LIVE THE LEADERNETIC

1. Why is it true that many people in our society don't view Christ in a positive way?

   ----

2. What are the five ways that you can effectively share Christ in your place of leadership?

NOTES

[1]Adapted from www.prudential.com, December 2004.

[3]Adapted from www.seattletimes.nwsource.com, December 2004.

[3]Kouses and Posner, *The Leadership Challenge* (Jossey Bass Publishers, Indianapolis, Ind., 1995), 20.

[4]Zig Ziglar, *Top Performance: How to Develop Excellence In Yourself and Others* (Berkley Publishing Group, Berkley, Calif., 1991), 32.

[5]www.turnto10.com/healthcheck10/1719168/detail.html, December 2004.

[6] www.barna.org, December 2004.

[7]Adapted from www.prudential.com, December 2004.

[8]Buckingham, Marcus and Donald Clifton, *Now, Discover Your Strengths* (New York: Free Press, 2001), 81.

[9]Taken from http://www.cnn.com/CNN/Programs/people/shows/tiger/profile.html

[10]Ana Dodson is a 2005 Prudential Spirit of Community Award winner. Her story was adapted from the Prudential website at www.prudential.com on October 21, 2005.

[11]Samuel Robinson is a 2005 Prudential Spirit of Community Award winner. His story was adapted from the Prudential website at www.prudential.com on October 28, 2005.

[12]Devin Cohen is a 2005 Prudential Spirit of Community Award winner. His story was adapted from the Prudential website at www.prudential.com on September 23, 2005.

[13]Jason Gonzales is a 2005 Prudential Spirit of Community Award winner. His story was adapted from the Prudential website at www.prudential.com on September 23, 2005.

[14]Adapted from an email by Jamie Smith of Utah, 2004.

Nexlead provides travel expeditions that enable Christian young leaders to use their passions to influence the future of society. Our vision is to see Christian young leaders shape the future.

Sign up for a Nexlead's EuroTrain expedition where you will:

- Learn from some of history's greatest leaders
- Gain leadership experience from incredible team ventures
- Get coaching and training from experienced leaders
- Experience culture in four of Europe's most amazing countries—England, Belgium, Switzerland, and France

You will walk away with:

- More confidence and increased leadership abilities
- Greater spiritual depth and maturity
- Focus and an understanding of your purpose in life
- Clarity about your future educational and career choices

Visit www.nexlead.org for more information.

Nexlead
PO Box 330517
Ft. Worth, Texas 76163
866-9-LEADER
www.nexlead.org
info@nexlead.org